CREDIT REPAIR

How to Instantly Boost Your Credit
Score!

By Glenn Nora

Table of Contents

document, including, but not limited to, — errors, omissions, or inaccuracies.

INTRODUCTION

Regardless of how bad your credit is, do not be embarrassed to deal with it. The fact is, there are millions of people just like you who have had financial difficulties.

Here are examples of a few people who had financial disasters and ruined credit, and they still came back:

In 1921 Walt Disney filed for bankruptcy in Missouri. That experience drove him west to start a new career in Hollywood animation. He then went on to create Disney Studios and Disneyland.

M.C. Hammer filed for bankruptcy in 1996. At his high point, Hammer was worth $33 million, but at the time of his bankruptcy, he had $1 million in assets and $10 million in debts. With a failing music career that could no longer bail him out financially, Hammer had to reinvent himself. Instead of performing, he began working with tech startups and new record labels, and now his credit is as good as ever.

Donald Trump filed for corporate bankruptcy four times, most recently in 2004 and 2009. He is now worth over $2 billion.

The bottom line is that it doesn't matter how bad your credit situation is. Your score and your financial situation can still improve.

Order your credit report and make a plan. It doesn't matter if your credit is already good and you want to make it better, or if it needs a lot of work. Figure out if there is a need for a dispute, and what you need to do to improve your score. Then decide how you will approach each issue.

Follow the advice in this book, including paying all bills on time, not trying to get too much credit at once, and paying down debt on credit cards.

Be proactive and periodically check your credit report. Look for unexpected negative or incorrect information, as well as traces of identity theft or fraud. Immediately dispute anything that should not be there.

Be patient. Of course, you want your credit to improve as soon as possible and we will go over some tips to do this, but some things may take longer than others. Stick to it, and over time, you will start to see positive results.

Get started. This is perhaps the most important piece of advice in this entire book. Many people have spent years drifting through life without understanding their credit score or how it affects their lives. They are clueless until they are denied a credit card or a home loan. You have a big advantage because you cared enough to buy this book, and with the tools in it, you can start improving your credit status TODAY. The sooner you start, the sooner your credit will improve. It is that simple.

CHAPTER 1: SHOCKING DETAILS ON HOW YOUR

CREDIT SCORE IS CALCULATED

Credit simply means your ability to borrow. As such, your credit score is a numerical representation of the risk a lender faces if they were to lend money to you. It is based on the analysis of one's credit files/history. Another layman's definition is that it is the difference between being denied credit and being granted credit.

Well, since money is often scarce, borrowing becomes a great option for sourcing funds to do whatever you want to do. It simply enables you to do things you would otherwise not afford if you were to be paying in cash. The credit score determines how lenders perceive you when advancing credit.

When your score is high, it means you are a reliable borrower so you won't need to pay more but when the score is low, the lenders treat you with caution and charge you more to advance credit to you. The cost of borrowing (interest you pay) is usually linked to your credit score. In other terms, the credit score determines how much you pay for a mortgage, health insurance, car insurance, and lots of other things including your utilities, cell phones, car payments, etc.

Employers also look into credit scores lately before hiring, which means this can determine whether you are hired or not. As you may have noticed, if your score is not good, your life can be pretty much a nightmare.

You will probably not even fathom the idea of living in your dream home, or driving your dream car because getting these will be literally out of your reach. Don't get me wrong, these people that run from their debts are not bad. Maybe they have a reason to stop paying off their debts. While a few missed payments may seem harmless, it actually does you permanent damage.

This damage becomes apparent when you try to borrow money from lenders, or when you get a new credit card. The fact that you missed some payments is permanently reflected in your credit score.

The Purpose of Credit Scores

Credit scores are designed to mitigate various types of risk. The most commonly mentioned risk is that of lending money to a borrower. It determines one's creditworthiness *i.e.* how lending money to you is risky. Here is a summary of why credit scoring is great.

- Credit scores allow people to get loans faster (almost instantly) since lenders can speed up the approval process. It is possible to make instant credit decisions if you are a lender, which means this helps borrowers to access credit fast.
- It is an objective way of making credit decisions: This focuses on facts rather than feelings which are unverifiable.
- There is more credit: Lenders approve more loans based on credit.
- Lower credit rates: There are more lenders (credit), which increases competition thus pushing the cost of credit lower.

Why should your credit score be high?
- Cheaper credit: Lenders are more willing to offer a lower interest rate. Here is a practical scenario:
- A credit score of 750 translates to a 6.11 interest on a 30 year $300,000 mortgage, while a credit score of 620 translates to a 7.42 interest on the same mortgage. As you can see, this difference will definitely translate into thousands of dollars over the 30year mortgage period.
- It puts you on an equal footing with creditors and lenders. You can comfortably negotiate knowing that lenders are competing to have you as their good risk borrower.
- In addition, businesses develop an interest in your business because it is a high-value asset courtesy of the low risk.
- Insurance companies also request your credit report before deciding your premiums or even whether they will cover the risk for you.

How a Credit Score is Calculated

Your FICO score is a measure of the overall quality of your credit. While it is not the only available metric for determining credit score, it is the one that is most commonly used by a wide range of different lenders and companies when it comes to determining the level of risk that is associated with a given individual.

The calculations that go into determining a person's credit score are proprietary which means that the Fair Isaac Company doesn't share them with anyone. However, some of the details regarding it have been found out, including the fact that a FICO score is based on a handful of different categories at various levels of importance to the total.

It has been determined that payment history is weighted with approximately 35 percent relevance, the amount owed has a 30 percent relevance, credit history length has a 15 percent relevance, abundance of new credit has a 10 percent relevance and the type of credit used has a 10 percent relevance.

Payment history relates to how prompt you have been when it comes to previous payments you have made to various creditors. It also factors in things such as delinquency, number of accounts you have in collections, bankruptcy and how long it has been since these problems appeared on your record. As such, the greater the number of problems you have had in this regard, the worse your overall FICO score is going to be.

When it comes to the amount you currently owe to lenders, FICO takes into account the amount of debt you currently have as well as the types of accounts you hold and the number of different accounts that you currently hold.

CHAPTER 2: DISCOVER HOW THE CREDIT SYSTEM WORKS

The credit system is made of consumers, financial companies, and credit bureaus. Three main credit bureaus gather and record information about your spending habits and credit history. TransUnion, Experian, and Equifax are the three most prominent and most often consulted credit bureaus.

If you have ever applied for a loan or some type of line of credit, one of these three companies likely provided the information that helped decide whether or not you got the line of credit. Your credit history includes payment history on accounts; applications for credit; credit card history; types of lines of credit; loan balances; and loan history.

Creditors whom you apply for credit, or have credit with, will electronically report information to these bureaus about every 30 days.

These bureaus will then store all of your credit information in your credit history so that future creditors can view your history and access your creditworthiness which is usually based on the amount of risk you represent. As competitors, the three main credit bureaus do not share credit information with each other, therefore, it is typical for the information that is represented in each report to be different.

Based on your credit history, creditors such as credit card companies, landlords, insurance companies, mortgage companies, schools, and auto loan lenders will review your credit information and use your history to decide whether or not to lend you money, and subsequently how much, for how long, and at what interest rate.

The better your credit history, the more likely creditors are to lend you money. Your credit history and credit score also determine the terms at which money will be made available to you.

When you apply for or borrow via installment loans (student or car loans) or through revolving credit (credit cards) the credit bureaus collect your credit information and calculate a credit score for you. Credit scores are determined by the types of credit accounts, the age of the accounts, debt usage, number of inquiries on your credit, and payment history.

Once this information is processed, you are given a FICO score in the range of 300850. FICO stands for Fair Isaac Corporation, which is a publicly-traded company that started in 1986 and introduced its' FICO score system in 1989.

The FICO score became popular in the late 1990's when Fannie Mae and Freddie Mac started requiring mortgage companies to use the FICO system as part of the loan underwriting process. The FICO score is generated by using a proprietary process using information from the credit bureaus, therefore, the credit bureaus are only responsible for gathering the information that is used in the FICO score using the FICO formula.

Credit applicants with scores in the range of 300579 are rated very poor, represent around 17% of the population, and typically are not approved for credit unless they leave a deposit or pay fees. Scores in the 580669-fair range, represent around 20.2% of the population and are considered subprime borrowers. Those in this range could be approved for lines of credit, but usually have to pay higher interest rates, because they are considered a higher risk.

Scores in 670739 good range, represent 21.5% of the population and are considered a lower risk as only 8% of applicants in this range will become seriously delinquent. People in this range have an improved lifestyle through purchases that are only possible with credit such as cars and houses.

They also enjoy services such as renting a car and having access to resources to pay for unexpected emergencies. Scores in the 740799 very good range, represent 18.2% of the population and are likely to receive better than average rates from lenders.

Scores in 800850 exceptional range, represent 19.9% of the population and get the best rates from lenders. People with credit in the last two ranges receive the best terms for borrowing money. They get more extensive credit lines, the lowest interest rates, a greater variety of available loans, and special offers for signing up with lenders. Banks compete for customers in these two groups by offering the best deals available because these customers will provide a steady income in loan fees with a lower risk of default.

It's much easier for your score to drop than it is for it to increase. A credit score of 760780 is ideal. The lower your credit score the more likely you are to default on debt. However, if your credit score is too high, as in above 780, it means you're not using your credit enough and you will start getting declined for credit because the banks won't be able to generate income from you. This is called a "high side override," which means you meet the creditor's requirements, but they still decline you.

Your credit score is also called your risk score. Lenders use it to assess whether or not you'll pay back debt as agreed. It's like a report card and the better your grades, the more likely it is you'll become a homeowner or get a new car. Your score varies up and down every time someone makes an inquiry on your credit history. Most of the information that is reported on your credit history expires and falls off your credit report in seven to ten years.

CHAPTER 3: LITTLE-KNOWN DETAILS ON YOUR CREDIT REPORT

What Is A Credit Report and What is in It

There is a lot of information on the credit report, and it can vary from person to person and across the credit bureaus. This is because creditors provide different types of data, at different times, and to various reporting agencies.

Also, everyone's credit history is changed (for instance a garnishment category may exist on one person's report because they had wages garnished, but the group may not even show up for someone who never had a garnishment). Because of this, I go into great detail explaining just about anything that might be found in a report.

For some people, this section can feel overwhelming, trying to figure it out. If that is your case, I recommend that you skip over areas that do not apply to you. And once you are familiar with this section, you can then come back and use it as a reference.

TIP: Credit reports contain information on the most recently reported activity from your creditors. If you recently made a payment and the story does not show the lower balance, it may be due to the creditor not having reported it yet. Very recent refunds may take a few days to record.

Credit reports vary by the agency producing them, but most of them are generally divided into six main sections with variations between the credit bureaus. Yours may have a different order or use different terminology. The six main sections are:

- Personal Information / Identifying Information / Consumer Statement / Employment
- Summary
- Account History / Account Information
- Public Information / Public Records
- Inquiries
- Creditor Contacts
- Personal Information / Identifying Information / Consumer Statement / Employment – this section is used to confirm your identity and contains basic information about you such as any names you may use, date of birth, current address, previous address, social security number, and employer information. None of this information is used in your credit score calculation but may be used by creditors to verify the information you submitted to them.

This section may also contain your "Consumer Statement." You are allowed to write a statement and ask the credit bureau to add it to your report. It usually explains a negative item on your story to a potential lender or creditor. For example, it may be something like this, "The 2013 Wells Fargo bank account was a shared account with my ex-wife." Your statement has no impact on your credit score.

Summary Section – this overview section has a categorized list of all your accounts on the credit report. There are nine categories in the summary section:

Total accounts – the total number of accounts on your statement, including both open and closed.

- Public accounts – number of accounts on your credit report listed as "open."
- Private accounts – number of accounts on your credit report listed as "closed."
- Delinquent – number of accounts listed as currently past due.
- Derogatory – number of accounts negatively impacting your credit score.
- Balances – the total amount of debt owed on all open and closed accounts on your credit report.
- Payments – total monthly payment amount you owe on all accounts.

Public Records – the number of public records listed on your credit report. This would include documents like bankruptcy filings, tax liens, and court judgments.

Inquiries – number of questions on your credit report from the last 24 months. These inquiries are recorded when a financial institution looks at your data for a credit application. Checking your credit report does not get recorded, nor does it impact your credit score.

Account History / Account Information – this section has detailed information about your credit accounts. The accounts are divided into five categories: real estate, installment, revolving, collection, and others.

- Real Estate – first and second mortgages.
- Installment – fixed-term accounts (nonreal estate) with regular payments like a car loan.
- Revolving – open term accounts with varying amounts like a credit card.

- Collection – very delinquent accounts that have been transferred to a collection agency, an attorney, or the creditor's internal collections department. They can include foreclosures, repossessions, and reports that have been charged off as well.

Other – accounts that don't fit in the different categories or their details are unknown. 30 Day accounts like an American Express card may be here.

What is Recorded in Each Account?

With each account, the report will list a summary of the terms and details, including the creditor name, account number, condition, balance, type, and pay status.

Creditor Name – the official account name. Because some companies are managed or owned by larger financial corporations, this may not be the name you expect or write your check to. In some cases, especially if it has gone to a collection agency, it may also be nonfinancial institutions such as a library, video rental or cable company, or even a cell phone company.

Account Number – the identifying number for your account. Usually, a portion of the name is hidden for security reasons. The report may indicate two numbers if this has gone to a collection agency, one for the collections and one for the original debt.

Condition – according to the most recent update from the creditor, the account will be open, closed, or paid off.

Balance – the amount currently owed on the account. This is based on the last reported activity from the creditor and may not be completely up to date. If the mind has gone to a collection agency, this will be the amount owed when it was transferred.

Type – common types include credit cards, cars, real estate, and student loans.

Pay Status – payment status according to the most recent update from the creditor. There will also be information about payment history over the past 24 months.

Past Due – the amount of payment overdue based on the most recent reports from the creditors.

High Balance – this is the most you have ever owed on the account. For a house, it would be the initial mortgage amount. For a credit card, it would be the most you ever charged on it.

Terms – this usually applies to loans and the number of payments scheduled. For instance, a 30-year home loan would show a repayment schedule of 360 months (30 years x 12 months).

Limits – the maximum amount you can borrow on this credit account.

Payment – the minimum amount you are required to pay each month.

Opened – the date the account was opened. If the mind has gone to a collection agency, this may be the date it was transferred.

Reported – the last time any activity took place on this account. Recent activity will not show up until it is published by the credit agency.

Responsibility – this is the type of trust you have for this account. For instance, it could be a joint, cosigner, or individual account.

Late Payments – details any late payments you have had over the last seven years.

Remarks – other notes about your account from the creditor. If the report has gone to a collection agency, it may have a statement like "The collection agency has been unable to locate the account holder" or "The account holder has never responded to requests from the collection agency."

TIP: When accounts are unpaid and sent to a collection agency, some of this information may get confusing. For instance, the date may change to the date the collection agency took over, as opposed to when the account was created. The account number may change, as well. To help with this, some reporting companies like TransUnion will list collection accounts separately.

Public Information / Public Records – this section contains publically available information affecting your credit and is usually limited to legal matters. These may include federal or state tax liens, bankruptcies, and judgments against you in civil cases.

- Three types of public records may show up in your credit report: bankruptcies, tax liens, and civil judgments.
- Bankruptcies – a legal filing that relieves a person of some or all of their debts. With a Chapter 13 bankruptcy, a portion of the debt is repaid and will stay on the credit report for seven years from the filing date. With a Chapter 7 bankruptcy, none of the debt is repaid, and it will remain on the credit report for ten years from the filing date.
- Tax Liens – a claim filed by any government tax agency against a person who they believe owes back taxes. An unpaid tax lien will remain on the credit report for ten years, while a paid tax lien will remain for seven years after the lien is paid.
- Civil Judgements – general category but is usually used to record judgment against you in a civil court.
- Others Occasionally, other public information related items may make their way to a credit report. They are rarely reported individually but may show up as part of another public record that gets reported, or as part of a remark added to your report by a creditor. They might include:
- Marital Items – could be any legal filing related to a marital or divorce issue.
- Financial Counseling – could be any public record indicating you have received financial counseling.
- Personal Property Liens – this is a type of lien usually filed when a loan is secured against personal property.

- ➢ Foreclosures – this record indicates a loan was defaulted on and the creditor has taken over the property.
- ➢ Garnishments – a court order to withhold some or all of a person's wages to repay a debt.

CHAPTER 4: SURPRISINGLY EASY WAYS TO MANAGING YOUR PERSONAL FINANCES

The Importance of Money Management

Do you find yourself with different credit cards, a mortgage, and an auto loan? There are methods to help you make this manageable. It takes time to discover the ins and outs of it and twist your budget so that it can satisfy your needs:

You know where your money is going

This is a huge benefit since it will allow you to watch the way you spend money and save more. You can track your spending for several months and then balance the budget to assign a lot of money to savings, or even retirement. If you handle your money well, you will manage to make early payments, and avoid surpassing the limit on the credit card. When you stick to your budget, these methods will assist you to save money.
This prevents you from spending much money.

A better plan of retirement

When you save now and manage your money in the right way, it will benefit you in the long term. First, it will force you to look into the future and look into your retirement plans. When you implement your money management skills, you will be building yourself a strong retirement plan. The money that you save and invest will grow as time goes by.

Allows you to concentrate on your goals

You will avoid unnecessary expenditure that doesn't support achieving financial goals. If you are dealing with limited resources, budgeting makes it complex to fulfill your ends.

You organize your spending and savings

When you divide your income into different types of expenditure and savings, a budget will allow you to remain aware of the type of expenditure that drains the portion of your money. This way, it is simple for you to set adjustments. Good money management acts as a reference for organizing receipts, bills, and financial statements. Once you organize all your financial transactions, you will save effort and time.

You can speak to your partner about money

If you do share your income with your spouse, then a budget can be the best tool to show how money is spent. This increases teamwork to work on a common financial target and prevents arguments on the way money is used. Creating a budget together with your spouse will help you to avoid conflict and eliminate personal conflicts on the way money is spent.

It determines whether you can take on debt and how much

Taking on debt isn't a bad thing, but it is important, especially if you cannot afford it. A budget will indicate the amount of debt load you can take on without getting stressed.

Budgeting

When you budget, you get the chance to single out and eliminate unnecessary spending such as on penalties, late fees, and interests. These little savings can increase with time.
A budget refers to a plan that takes into account your monthly cash flow and outflow. This is a snapshot of what you own, and what you expect to spend, and which will allow you to realize your financial goals by assisting you in highlighting your saving and spending.

Creating a budget is the most crucial aspect of financial planning. The amount of money you have doesn't indicate how much money you make, but instead, it is how effective your budgeting is. If you want to take care of your finances, then you will have to understand where your money is flowing to. Contrary to popular belief that budgeting is hard, it isn't, and it doesn't eliminate the fun from your life. A budget will save you from an unexpected financial crisis and a life of debt.

Monitor your expenses and income

The first thing to building a budget is to determine the amount of money you have and what you are spending it on. By monitoring your expenses, you will manage to classify how you spend your money. Planning how you spend your money is critical because you can tell how much you want to spend in every category. You can monitor your income and expenses by creating a journal, spreadsheet, or cash book. Every time you make money, you can monitor it as income, and every time you spend money, you can track it as an expense. If you use a debit card, try to track back three months of your spending to get a comprehensive picture of your expenditure.

Evaluate your income

The next stage is to assess your income. You can do this by computing the amount of income you get via gifts, scholarships, *etc.*

Determine your expenses

Once you know your monthly income, next is to determine the total of your expenses. First, you need to define what your fixed, variable expenses are. Fixed expenses, sales, and bills have the same price every month. The fixed expenses comprise of car payments, internet, and rent. Variable expenses refer to costs that change, such as utilities and groceries.

Be sure to include payments of debt in your budget. Find out the amount that you can contribute towards your debts to make sure that you are on the correct path to financial stability. Handling debts and savings go hand in hand.

Building a Saving Strategy

It is quite easy to forget to save money. Keep in mind that you always pay yourself first. Give it a try using 1020% of your income savings. Since savings increase, you can choose to include money that you didn't spend in the budget to save.

Many people know how to manage the little money they get when the month ends, but they find it hard to save when they have a tight budget. If you look at finance articles online, you will see different types of saving methods—right from freezing all spending to packing your own lunch for a month. But how can you determine which one's work? In this section, you will learn easy money-saving strategies you can implement and how you can make them work for you:

Stay out of debt

Being debt-free will help you to save cash; if you can pay off all your debt, you will get the chance to organize your debt. The stats on eliminating debt can be shocking. For example, the Claris poll showed that only 22% of people attempted this strategy, and 26% reported that it worked for them. In other words, this strategy can help you save money. Staying out of debt can save you a good sum of cash, but many people find it hard to pay off their debts.

Be a Minimalist

Adopting a minimalist approach is a type of voluntary simplicity. It requires a person to cut down on costs so that they concentrate on what is important. A minimalist's life generally means owning a smaller house, fewer "toys", and fewer clothes. But it also implies minimal work and more time to do the things that you like.

This is a great saving strategy that works even for those who don't want to use it. A minimalist approach can be the effect of other methods to save. In most cases, many people scaled their life to stick to their budget. Then, with time, they discovered that their simple lifestyle helped them save more.

There are various misconceptions about minimalism. A blog about minimalism jokes that minimalists live in small apartments and don't have jobs, cars, TVs, or more than 100 objects.
The purpose of minimalism is to free yourself from issues in life that aren't important. It is not focused on sacrifice; it merely involves eliminating things that you don't want to have in life or creating room for things that you care about. As a result, living with fewer items can make you feel satisfied.

If you aren't sure whether you can deal with this kind of life, you can start small and slowly identify a few things in your life that you don't want. For example, if your wardrobe is filled with many things, perhaps throw out or donate some clothes. Or if you spend a lot of time online, plan to reduce your screen time.

Whatever you decide to do, make sure that you don't simplify your life by surrendering on the things you value or treasure; instead, choose things that require the most work for the least reward.
If you are searching for methods to help you save a lot of money, these methods are the best ones, to begin with. Since they have worked for other people, there is a big chance that they will work for you too. However, make sure that you don't jump in and try all the methods at once—just select strategies that you believe may work for you.

Investing your Money

Investing your money gives you a chance to grow your money, and even make more than what you have. However, not everyone who decides to invest their money makes profits; some have lost tons of money in the process. There is a different way to invest your money, and this section will introduce you to some of the most common strategies for investment: Online investing can be a quick and convenient method that is more affordable than other methods. But before you can handle your online investment, you need to ask yourself several questions:

Online investing is designed for everyone. By choosing this option, you hold the responsibility to research all investments and make all investment decisions regarding your online account. If you don't feel okay as that kind of investor, you could be comfortable working with a financial advisor. If you like to manage your investment portfolio and feel secure that you have enough knowledge, you may decide to go with online investment.

Stop Spending

If you can't stop spending money that you don't have, this book will only temporarily fix your problems, if it is even able to do that. If you have a habit of living out of your means and buying things you cannot afford, this is your chance to fix that. If you want to fix your credit and improve your life financially, you must take care of these things. So, sit tight, make a budget, and find something that works, and cut up those maxed out credit cards if you have to.

CHAPTER 5: PROVEN MINDSET FOR

CREDIT MANAGEMENT

Whenever you want to overcome something, you need to make sure that you are in the right mindset to do so. By doing this, you will be able to mentally overcome your challenge and keep yourself from making the same mistake
.

Tips to Help Reach the Right Mindset to Get out of Debt

1. Realization Of Your Current Mindset

Before you start to make any changes, you need to know where your mindset sits at this moment. Think of how you feel when you ponder about your credit card debt as this will tell you more about your mindset than you might realize. If you are like most people, you feel frustrated about your current situation. How you got into credit card debt will depend on what you are saying to yourself.

For example, you might be angry or blame yourself for getting into debt. You might ask yourself why you allowed this situation to happen.
No matter what you notice about your current mindset, you need to accept it and understand why you feel this way. You also need to understand that it is okay for you to feel like this as it will help you reach the get out of debt mindset.

2. Debt Is Not a Burden, It Is an Obstacle

There is a difference between a burden and an obstacle. When you have a burden, you have to deal with it; there is no way around it. However, there is a way around an obstacle. Therefore, you need to look at debt as an obstacle. It is something that you can overcome with the right steps. It is also something that you can keep yourself from getting into again.

Take a moment to think of ways that you can work toward erasing your credit card debt as an obstacle. For example, if you have a $75 minimum monthly payment that you have been making, how much is going toward interest and fees? If you notice that this amount is $35, see what you can do to increase your monthly payment to $110. This will allow you to pay more than your minimum payment. More importantly, it will also allow you to put $75 toward your balance with half of your amount toward fees and the other half toward your balance.

3. Don't Forget About Gratitude

Debt can cause us to become resentful. We often see other people enjoy the luxuries of life, whether it is by purchasing a new vehicle or going on a vacation. You might even feel resentful because they can afford new clothes. One of the best ways to get out of the negative mindset that is attached to credit card debt is to let go of your resentment and focus on gratitude.

Look around your home to see all the wonderful items that you own. Try to think about how lucky you are when it comes to your family, friends, and everyone else who is in your life. You don't always need to focus on the bigger things; sometimes looking at the smaller moments is just as helpful. For example, you may feel gratitude when your child smiles at you while they are playing quietly with their toys.

If you struggle with gratitude, one of the best techniques is writing down what you are grateful for at the end of every day. Find a journal and discuss everything that made you feel positive. You can also discuss what bad things happened, but try to find a way you can learn from them or turn them into something a little positive.

4. Take Responsibility For Your Debt

There is a big difference between blaming yourself for your credit card debt and taking responsibility for it. The biggest difference is what type of mindset you are in. For instance, if you are asking yourself how you could have been so dumb to allow yourself to obtain so many credit cards, you are blaming yourself for what happened. Instead, you need to take responsibility, which means you should try saying something like this to yourself: "I know I got myself into credit card debt because I took out too many credit cards. Now, how can I start to pay off my credit card debt?"

Taking responsibility helps put you in the right mindset because it helps you realize that while you made a mistake, you understand the error, and you are ready to solve the problem. On top of this, you should always look at how you can keep yourself from making the same mistake again. No matter how you get yourself out of credit card debt, they are always going to be tempting.

5. *Stop Seeing Debt Free as a Solution to Your Problem*

Another step you want to take to prepare yourself for your mindset to get out of debt is to stop looking at becoming debt-free as the solution to your problem. The reality is that there is probably more than one reason for why you are in debt. While you want to avoid blaming yourself, you also need to take responsibility for your mistakes.

Therefore, write down all the ways that you can become free of debt. This might mean that you should close all your credit cards and work on a plan to pay them off on time, or it may also mean that you should get a second job to help pay off your debt quickly. Instead of thinking about becoming debt-free as the only solution, you need to think of it as the outcome. You need to make becoming debt-free or having financial freedom be your ultimate goal. You should work on coming up with a series of steps that will help you reach your goal.

For example, let's assume that you're a college student who has opened up five credit cards. You are soon graduating and know that you need to start paying off all your smaller debt because you will be paying off student loans in the very near future. Therefore, you decide that one of your best options is to pay off your credit cards and no longer allow yourself to use them. Therefore, you work to think about how you can pay off your five credit cards in a single year.

At the moment, you only have a part-time job working at Applebee's restaurant. You start your budget where you write down your income and any bills that you have. You notice that even after paying all your bills, you still have at least $150 to $200 of your income available.

You then look at your other spending habits, such as how often you eat out and what type of food you buy, and you decide on ways that you can reduce your spending, which increases your amount from $150 to $275. You then decide that this is a livable amount for you, at least until you can get a fulltime job.

Next, you think about all the tips you receive from your job as a waitress. Typically, you bring home anywhere from $100 to $300, depending on the night and how busy it is. You realize that you can put all your tip money toward paying off your credit cards. This will allow you to pay off your debt faster.

After doing the math, you realize that all your credit cards will be paid off in full by the time your student loans will begin needing to be paid. Through your planning, you started to see becoming debt free from credit cards as your outcome instead of your solution. By doing this, you were able to come up with a logical solution that works, provided that you can follow it over the course of the year.

Your Get out of debt Mindset

There is no direct mindset to help you get out of debt. Instead, you need to find a mindset that will allow you to stay positive and focused. This will also help you to remain financially free once you reach this point. In general, the following steps are ways that you can build your own get out of debt mindset.

Set a Game Plan and Stick to It

You need to create goals and create your plan of action to get out of debt. While you don't have to write your plan down, this is always a good idea as it will help you remain focused on what you need to do. For example, you know that you have five credit cards which are all maxed out. In fact, you are close to going over the limit on most of them, which will make the credit card company charge you an over the limit fee.

You realize that this will only create a larger amount of credit card debt. Therefore, you decide that you need to pay more than your minimum payment on these credit cards first.

Then, once you have made those credit card limits lower, you decide that you will pay more on the credit cards which show the lowest amount. This will allow you to at least get two out of your five credit cards paid off within six months. From there, you will be able to take the money you don't need for those two credit cards and split that sum between your other three credit cards. Through this plan, you realize that within two years, you will be completely free of credit card debt.

Sometimes we struggle more with the fact that we need to stick to our plan, especially when it comes to money. For example, you might find yourself in an emergency when your car breaks down. While you have some money saved, you don't have enough. Typically, one of the first bills people stop paying in this situation is their credit cards.

This is because many people rank credit card payments as one of the least important payments they have to make. Of course, this thought tends to change once they find themselves with higher credit card debt due to missed payments and fees for being over their limit.

The biggest solution to this problem is to set a budget. Create a budget that includes your credit card payments and doesn't allow yourself to push your budget aside because you have an emergency. Instead, look at your other options, such as short-term loans or asking friends or family for help. Above all, you need to stay focused on your goals; this is the only way to ensure that you will not allow yourself to break your budget agreement.

Reframe Your Thoughts

Another major step for your mindset to get out of debt is to turn your negative thoughts into positive ones. This is one of the biggest reasons that you want to become grateful for what you have in life, including your credit card debt. Even though this might be hard to do right now, it is important to realize that this is a life lesson you are learning. In fact, by taking control of your credit card debt, you will be able to take control of your budget and reach financial freedom. Furthermore, the more negative you are, the less likely you will be to follow your goals and your budget.

There are several steps you can use to start to reframe your thoughts. For example, you could write down your problem, and you can then jot down your thoughts about your credit card debt. From there, you can include at least three emotions you feel associated with your credit card debt; these emotions can be fear, anxiety, stress, or anger.

For the next step, you will want to reframe your thoughts by turning them into something positive. You will need to write down evidence to support these positive thoughts. Then, you will write down at least three emotions that are associated with your positive thoughts.

Write down a List of Reasons to Get out of Debt

Getting out of credit card debt is not going to be easy. In fact, you will need to take steps to keep you focused as there will be times you feel frustrated or lack confidence in getting out of debt. One of the ways to overcome this is by writing down a list of reasons for wanting to get out of debt. This list can include anything that comes to your mind. For example, you might write that you want to own a home one day.

You might also state that you want to be debt-free within two years. Another reason might be your children will be going to college starting in five years, and you want to be able to help them. It doesn't matter what your reasons are; what really matters is that they are your reasons for getting out of debt.

Realize That People Depend on You

If you have a family, you will want to think about all the people who depend on you for your income. It is a lot easier to be able to go out and buy diapers, groceries, and any other household items you need when you don't have to worry about what debt you are getting into. Instead, you can pay through your debit card or with cash without having to worry about the purchase again.

Another reason you should think about the people that depend on you is that they will give you the motivation to follow through with your debt free credit card plan and work toward keeping yourself free of debt.

Set up Automatic Payments

Every credit card company will allow you to set up automatic payments through their website. Some will even set up automatic payments while over the phone. Whatever you need to do, take the time to set up these payments. This will help you make sure that these bills are getting paid. The trick is that you want to refrain from canceling or postponing your automatic payments as this is typically an option. Again, this is something that you can put into your plan so you are less likely to cancel.

Find Ways to Keep You Motivated

While you are creating your get out of debt plan, you want to include ways that will help you stay motivated. Perhaps this means checking your progress every other month to see how much your credit card debt has gone down. For example, if you have five credit cards and you are paying $100 on them every month, you will see they have gone down close to $200 every two months. If you add this up, you have decreased your total credit card debt by $1,000. You can decide to track your progress through a spreadsheet on your computer or via a journal. Note the amount you owe when you pay and then notice the new amount the next time you make a payment.

Know That You Can Do It

Sometimes we struggle to follow through with our debt-free plan because we feel like we can't achieve it. It is important to note that there will be times you feel this way. There will be moments when you feel like you can't continue to focus on paying off your debt. You might look and see that you still have two years of credit card debt to pay off and that your other bills continue to pile up.

It is important to realize that everyone has these moments. They are ones where self-doubt pops up in our minds and continues to try to push us to fall back into our old ways. When these times happen to you, the best thing you can do is acknowledge them and then tell yourself that if other people can do it, so can you. You don't want to push these feelings to the side because they will only continue to crawl back into your mind; in fact, they will start coming to you more often.

Another way to look at this part of your mindset is to change your "I can't" to "I can". Then, whenever you think or state a phrase like "I can't pay off all this credit card debt within two years", you will switch your mindset and instead state "I can pay off all this credit card debt in two years".

Establish a Reward System

The fact is you will find yourself struggling to maintain your mindset to get out of debt from time to time. This might not be because you want to purchase something that you can't afford, but rather it may be because you find yourself getting tired of seeing how much money you owe toward credit cards.

One of the best ways to keep you from feeling this way is to establish a reward system that will help you stay on task. When you are working on your get out of debt plan, write down what milestones you want to focus on and then reward yourself for reaching these milestones. For example, you may decide that every time you have paid off $500 on each credit card, you decide to take a couple of hours to do something fun.

The trick is you want to make sure that whatever you decide to do, you save it for your reward system. For example, if you decide that you will watch a couple of episodes of your favorite Netflix television show, the rewards won't work as well if you find yourself doing this randomly throughout your day.

CHAPTER 6: INSTANTLY FIX YOUR

CREDIT NOW!

If you are affected by bad credit, remember it happens to a lot of people. Credit repair will require a lot of effort and it is a process that can span out over the course of many months, but in the end, it's worth it. It's possible that a credit repair will not make all your financial problems go away and you may still be confronted with some bad credit "symptoms" that will stay on your credit report.

These problems usually require long term attention, but can be minimized over time so much so that even if you have or had them, your credit will still be considered good. I will try to explain credit repairing as best as I can so that it can be accessible to everyone

The first step for fixing your credit is doing your homework. This involves a bit of research, but it can be done in a few hours or days, depending on the time you allocate daily to this problem. What you must do is get copies of your credit reports from more than one agency. Two or three are the best option. Compare your credit reports and pick out the problems you find that are important or predominant. After you identify what causes your credit to be in such bad shape, try to write down why each negative point is the way it is.

The importance of correctly identifying the problems cannot be stressed enough. Once you find out what led to the negative items on credit reports, try to reason with yourself. Why should each one of them be eliminated? With a clear motive and a clear perspective on each problem, a lot of the work is already done and you can move on to searching for solutions.

These will come more easily since you now know what your bad credit is based on and why you need to remove certain problems. Setting clear and realistic goals is a step that is widely used in fixing any problem, not just financial difficulties.

You may find that some of the issues in the credit reports may be incorrect or have already been remedied, in which case you should contact the agency that put together your credit report and explain your point of view. Reporting agencies can't know what happens in your life daily and even though they keep an updated database, it takes time to do it so they will appreciate your clarification.

Keep in mind that you have to make time to do some investigative work of your own. But how will I be able to analyze all this information correctly if I don't have any experience in finance? Not all reports will look the same, which is why you should be provided with the necessary information to decode them.

You should pay special attention to the fields which show which payments are up to date, defaulted or late because there you will also find the reason why they've inserted each negative entry. You should also pay special attention to the time the account was opened, information on monthly payments and credit limit. Of course, any incorrect information will easily be corrected and if that scratches a few items off your list, that's a happy case

Follow these Strategies to Fix your Credit

Delete inquiries

In this strategy, you agree to pay a creditor only if they agree to delete such items from the credit report. I mentioned zero balances; don't fall for the trap of creditors who say they will mark it as zero. Zero is not good for you because it shows you have been having problems in the past (this sticks in your credit report for 7 or more years)! If the information passes to collection agencies after 2 years, you can also use this strategy to make them stop reporting your settled debt. In any case, they buy the debts for a tiny fraction so anything they get will probably be good enough! This is the best time (when the debt is with the collection agencies) to use the pay to delete strategy because you have more bargaining power. If the collection agency doesn't accept your offer, its only option is through judgment.

Note#1: Use pay to delete when you start noticing new derogatory items in your report since these could easily hurt your credit. You might even start seeing multiple collection companies reporting the same debt. In such times, you have an advantage since you negotiate everything on your terms; if one does not accept your offer, another will definitely take it.

Note#2: Have everything put in writing if they agree on your terms. If they cannot put it in writing, don't pay. After paying, you should give it about 45 days to reflect in your credit report. Don't take anything less than deletion. Don't accept updating the balance. If they cannot delete, don't pay. The process is pretty fast so they shouldn't give you excuses that they cannot delete. Mention the Universal Data Form to let them know that you know that it is possible.

Note#3: Choose your battles well *i.e.* Do not use this strategy on creditors who have a lot to lose because they might sue you to compel you to pay. Aim for creditors who have already been barred by the statute of limitations (2 years have passed), which means they cannot sue you in court to compel you to pay.

Identify theft claim
This is definitely a large population so anyone could be a victim. If you are sure that your score has been ruined because of identity theft, you can use this method. Abusing this method could land you into trouble with the law. Here is how to dispute using the method:

- Step 1: Report to the police because you will need this report later
- Step 2: File the dispute with FTC
- Step 3: Go on to dispute with various credit bureaus.
- Step 4: Set up an identity theft alert (be sure to know what this means in terms of your access to credit).

Look out for errors in the report

I mentioned that 93% of credit reports have been proven to have errors. Look out for any of these then file a dispute. Such things as the last date of activity, write off date, wrong account name or number and others could be enough to taint your credit. Don't overlook any of that. If the report really has an error, don't be discouraged by the credit bureau's stalling tactics.

Mention the Notice (Summons) and complaint to let them know that you are really aware of what the law requires of them. The bureaus wouldn't want to have their systems investigated and proven to be weak/flawed so this strategy can actually compel them to correct errors thus boosting your credit.

Pay the original creditor

You don't want multiple collection agencies reporting new items every month since this hurts your score. Simply send a check with full payment of the outstanding amount to the original creditor. Then send proof of the payment to the collection agencies that have reported that debt. After that, you then request that they should delete all the derogatory items from your credit report. You can blend this with the pay to delete the strategy mentioned above.

Request for proof of the original debt

If you are sure that the credit card has been written off due to late payment, there are times when the carriers might not have the original billing statements within 30 days as stipulated by the law. With this, you can get the item removed from your report so that it appears as if the entry was never there. You can also request the original contract that you actually signed when applying for a credit card.

Settle your debt

Total debt owed accounts for up to 30% of the credit score so don't overlook this. This includes personal loans, car loans, and credit utilization. You should also calculate the credit utilization ratio (the balance you carry in your revolving fund compared to your credit). To pay your debts, you can use snowballing or avalanching strategies.

Snowballing involves paying off debts with the lowest balance first then closing them as you move up to the bigger debts. Avalanching involves paying debts starting from those with the highest interest rates as you move down.

Settle your bills promptly

You could even set up automatic payments just to ensure that you won't miss payments since the amounts are deducted from your account. The biggest contributors to this include collections, bankruptcies, and different late payments. You should note that the recent delinquencies have a greater effect than old ones; 70% of the score is determined by whatever has happened within the past 2 years.

Contact with the creditor

At this point, you have to write another letter, this time to the creditor. You can continue claiming that the negative information is wrong, but be warned that they will not believe you if you do not provide solid proof to back up your claim. If you don't think you can muster up that proof to make a good case for reestablishing your good credit, I suggest you consider a different route.

You can write to the creditor and express the fact that you are concerned about the issue affecting your good credit and even though you are aware that the negative item is based on accurate facts, you want to find a solution that will work for both parties involved. This way, you announce your intent of repairing your credit politely and professionally, so they might be more predisposed towards collaborating with you in finding a more suitable solution.

Handling Disputes for Delinquent Accounts

The main methods of improving your score from this point involve disputing and removing negative information, and managing your current credit accounts. If this is your first look at this, chances are that you have a few incorrect items showing up on one of your reports. That is not a problem because we are going to get them removed! Everyone is entitled to dispute incorrect information on his or her credit report, and by law, the credit bureau has to look into it in a timely manner (usually 30 days.)

Now if this is an account that shows an amount due but actually has a zero balance, you can always get it removed from your record. Occasionally you may have to get proof of a zero balance, but this is rare.

Ok, so gather all the incorrect information in front of you. Remember that this can be anything, from misspelled names to incorrect dates or amounts. There are two methods of disputing, and people will recommend either one. Your options are to file a dispute online or mail a dispute letter by certified mail.

Filing a dispute online is simple and quick, which is why I prefer it. You can file many disputes in a short period of time. In fact, "credit repair" companies will usually just dispute everything, hoping the creditors simply don't respond with the correct information. How far you want to take this tactic is completely up to you. Disputes can usually be filed at the same time and must be done individually with each bureau showing incorrect information.

On each bureau's website, find the online dispute button and follow the instructions. After you pick the appropriate items to dispute, enter the correct information, usually with a brief description of what you are disputing, and when you are done you will be provided with a reference/dispute number. Write this number down! You will need it to check back in on your report and make sure the dispute is removed.

Tracking Your Credit Progress

Before you go out in the world and start applying for more credit, let's get a better idea of your numerical score. There are two easy ways to do this for free. The first is to sign up for *www.creditkarma.com*. It is free and quick, just put in your standard info. It is not necessary to link your checking accounts or any bank information to use the service, but it is offered as a financial management tool if you desire it.

With Credit Karma, be aware that this is not an exact score, it is an estimation based on the data that the website has available. You may notice it is normally accurate, but sometimes it is off by just a little, or lags by a week or two. The actual FICO score itself can vary by as much as 2050 points but is normally within

20 points or so. Use Credit Karma as a guide more than anything.

Several other free sites are similar but do not quite offer the scope of services that Credit Karma does. You are welcome to explore them all, just be wary of entering credit card or bank information.

The other way to get your numerical credit score is through credit card services. At the time of this writing, a few major banks offer your FICO score through having a credit card account with them, including Barclays, Discover, and Capital One. This is always changing, but the current trend suggests that more companies will start to offer this service.

Pay bills promptly

Most lending companies refer only to payment history in assessing whether a potential borrower is creditworthy or not. As such, to repair your credit score, you must pay your bills immediately, and you must do so promptly and on time. One must remember that a bad payment history decreases the chance that his or her application will be accepted. Paying bills promptly also repairs your credit score.

In paying your bills, debts, and obligations, you may choose to consider the following order of priority:
- Pay first those secured by real and personal properties because they can be lost if he fails to pay them on the due date.
- Next, pay those that have high-interest rates to prevent these charges from accumulating over time.

- Next, pay those that have high amounts because these require a large amount of money.
- After these three debts are paid, he may choose to divide his remaining money to partially pay his other debts.

Paying bills promptly and on time also increases the length of your credit history because it prevents your accounts from being closed due to delinquency in payment.

Maintain a low debt on credit cards

One must take note that having a high amount of debt decreases the chance that your credit application will be granted. Maintaining a low debt on credit cards also repairs your credit score. A person can maintain a low debt on credit cards either by paying his bills or by reducing the amount that he spends on his purchases. A suggested practice is for him to pay his credit card bills twice a month and making a list of what he needs to purchase (creating a budget is very helpful).

Avoid having a high outstanding debt

In relation to maintaining a low debt on credit cards, a person must also avoid having a high outstanding debt because it creates a negative impact on the credit score. To prevent this from happening, he may pay these debts partly based on the amount of money that he has, or he may negotiate with his creditors for a possible settlement of these debts.

Most of the time, lending companies accept partial debt payment because it prevents their borrowers from running due to the inability to pay. If feasible, he should resort to this method so he can slowly decrease his outstanding debt.

Get new accounts only when needed.

A person must get new accounts only when needed and only when his or her financial resources permit them to do so. Getting many accounts at one time negatively affects your credit score, especially when you started using a certain amount of credit for each account because it means that in paying your bills, your financial resources will be divided among these accounts.

Make payment reminders

In promptly paying his bills and debts, a person must make payment reminders. These are small notes that contain various debts that he has to pay, the amount that he needs to spend for every debt, and the frequency through which he needs to make the payment. Making payment reminders helps him a lot in managing his financial resources because it lets him prioritize paying the debt first before allocating his money to something else.

The best time to make payment reminders is when making a budget. A budget is a summary of the sources of revenue and an itemized list of the expenses of a person within a specified period of time, usually for a month. As he lists the items in his budget, he may immediately allocate some of his money in paying his existing debts.

Focus on the credit report. Not the score

Remember, your credit score is just a number, and even though an important number, don't focus on it just yet if you have some repairing or rebuilding to do. Once you get to the point where you have done all you can do to remove anything reporting as derogatory, you will then have the fun part of building or rebuilding your credit. With no negative information and no positive information reporting your score will remain low and it's possible you may have no score at all.

We have all heard "No credit is bad credit", but no credit is only a small step away from great credit. Focus on your credit report, it is the determining factor that shows how much you should be trusted, and how much previous creditors have trusted you, this speaks the highest in their decisions.

Maintain a High Credit Score

While doing your credit repair and after achieving a high score, you keep track of the changes, be it progress or decrease. You can ask this from a credit reference agency. This might entail money. Nowadays, there are credit tracking sheets available online for free. You have to make sure that they are trustworthy, though.

Going back to economizing, one way to do this is by using energy-efficient appliances. It is not ideal to buy an appliance based on the price alone. You might be getting an appliance for a low price but you might not have realized that you are getting less than you paid for in terms of quality and reliability.

Aside from that, cheaper appliances often consume more electricity. In the long run, you will not have actually saved anything. Aside from saving electricity and money, you have to save water as well. Use only the amount of water that you need.

Preparation is also worth noting in maintaining a high credit score. Unwanted events in the future such as redundancy, moving out, accidents, illnesses, calamities, and death are worth preparing for. You can apply for insurance for these events. Nevertheless, you should still prepare because of the possibility of noncoverage from your insurance premiums.

When it comes to your financial activities, the right attitude would be living in accordance with your financial capacities. Do not be obsessed with materials that you will not be using. Spend your finances for your needs. It does not mean that you should not enjoy your money. As a matter of fact, recreation and rest form part of your needs. All you have to do is to use your money wisely. Treat yourself in a way that you are not incurring debts or lessening your savings.

CONCLUSION

You should now have a better idea of how to repair your credit with or without using section 609. While many people feel that this is one of the best ways to get rid of your bad credit, there are a lot of situations where writing a dispute letter will not help you gain better credit.

For example, if you have missed payments on your credit cards within a certain amount of time. Even if the credit card company states that you didn't pay during the months you did, this is something that won't work to dispute because you have recently missed payments.

When it comes to struggling with credit card debt, the best way to start repairing your credit is to make sure you understand the federal laws associated with credit card debt. Make sure that you have been protected and that the credit card company didn't do anything illegally. If everything is legal, then you simply want to work on paying off your credit card payments.

You will want to come up with a financial plan which will help you start to pay off your credit cards strategically. You then want to make sure that, no matter what, you follow this plan. Even if you find yourself in an emergency after a few months when your car breaks down, you want to find another way to come up with your emergency funding.

It is important that you continue to make more than the minimum payment on time with all your credit cards. The fewer fees you need to add to your balance, the quicker you will be able to pay off your credit card debt.

Another way to bring down credit card debt quickly, especially if you are overdrawn and missed a few payments, is to contact the credit card company. While many people don't realize this, most credit card companies want to work with you. The number one reason for this is they want to keep you as a customer, basically, so they can continue receiving your money.

One strategy to use is to call and say that you would like to close your account. They will then try to focus on keeping your account open, which usually results in them dropping a few missed payments or over the limit fees. Another strategy to use is simply to explain to them what happened, why you were late, and tell them that you want to put your account in good standing. They are usually willing to drop some fees or so much money if you are willing to pay a certain amount off that day.

If you decide to write a dispute letter under section 609 because you have noticed that information which reflects negatively on your credit score is over seven years old, then you should follow the tips and guidelines within chapters five and six. You want to make sure that you do your best when writing this letter.
Don't feel that it is just a simple letter and write it quickly. Make sure that you have all the information you need, all the documentation, you proofread the letter, and certify the letter with a receipt request. You also want to make sure that you document everything.

Keep all the correspondence that you receive and that you send, keep your original copies, and anything else. You want to have a thorough paper trail.

Finally, take time to imagine your financial freedom.

After almost four years, you have paid off all of your credit card debt. While your credit history will remain on your credit report until the seven years are up, you have noticed that your credit score is increasing. You have noticed that you are less stressed and you no longer ignore your phone when a number you do not recognize is calling.

You have decreased the number of credit cards you own from five to one. The one credit card you have only had a credit limit of $1,000 which is something you know that you can pay off within a few months if you have to use your credit card for an emergency. Until then, you have it safely stored away, which makes you usually forget that you still have a credit card for emergencies.

You also have a set budget that you follow every month. This includes ways that you are increasing your emergency fund, so you can think about safely closing your last credit card account and no longer even have credit cards on your mind. With every credit card offer you receive in the mail; you immediately shred and then recycle the paper. You are living comfortably and growing your savings. You have finally reached financial freedom.

Thank You

I would like to thank you from the bottom of my heart for coming along with me on this credit repair journey. There are many investing books out there, but you decided to give this one a chance.

If you liked this book, then I need your help!

Please take a moment to leave an honest review for this book. This feedback gives me a good understanding of the kinds of books and topics readers want to read about and it will also give my book more visibility.

www.ingramcontent.com/pod-product-compliance
Lightning Source LLC
Chambersburg PA
CBHW071518210326
41597CB00018B/2812